MAGIC STORY

THE
MAGIC
STORY

Frederick van
Rensselaer Dey

MEDIA

Published by Gildan Media LLC
aka G&D Media.
www.GandDmedia.com

The Magic Story was originally published in 1900.
G&D Media edition 2021.
Introduction copyright © 2021 by Mitch Horowitz.

Cover design by David Rheinhardt of Pyrographx

Interior design by Meghan Day Healey of Story Horse, LLC.

ISBN: 978-1-7225-0544-8

"If you have skill, apply it; the world must profit by it, and, therefore, you."

could get straight A's, or *could* excel at work, or *could* find a positive relationship ... if only they were able to freely throw themselves upon the energies of their higher, better, more formidable doppelgänger, waiting to be released. This possibility is real, but it is rarely, or only fleetingly, exercised.

Many modern fiction writers and psychologists, not to mention their ancient and folkloric forebears, have posited the existence of this "other self." Psychologist Carl Jung famously called it the shadow, which he identified as a fount of unacknowledged desires and proclivities; if acknowledged and integrated into your day-to-day consciousness, these shadow traits could lead to the growth of untapped powers, confidence, and abilities. For fantasy writer Robert Louis Stevenson, the other self was the malevolent

"Mr. Hyde," a feral counterpart to the refined and approachable persona of Dr. Jekyll. For Edgar Allan Poe, the other side was represented by "William Wilson," the title of Poe's 1839 short story in which his protagonist, the debauched Wilson, grows up alongside an uncanny double who shares his name, appearance, and birthdate, and who eventually turns out to be the maleficent hero's alienated conscience.

Many fiction writers, like Stephen King in his 1989 novel, *The Dark Half*, see the other self as a figure of repressed violence and evil. But that reflects only one sliver of the split-self riddle of human nature. More important for our purposes, your counter-self can be a figure of relative fearlessness, effectiveness, and ability. Author Napoleon Hill highlighted these possibilities in his 1937 self-help classic, *Think and Grow*

Introduction

————◊————

Rich. (A book that you do yourself a disservice by not reading if you permit yourself to be put off by its seemingly gauche title.) Hill wrote:

> *O. Henry discovered the genius which slept within his brain, after he had met with great misfortune, and was confined to a prison cell in Columbus, Ohio. Being FORCED, through misfortune, to become acquainted with his "other self," and to use his IMAGINATION, he discovered himself to be a great author instead of a miserable criminal and outcast. Strange and varied are the ways of life, and stranger still are the ways of Infinite Intelligence, through which men are sometimes forced to undergo all sorts of punishments before discovering their own brains, and their*

own capacity to create useful ideas through imagination.

One of the oddest inspirational works ever written, *The Magic Story*, reprinted here from one of its earliest extant editions, featured this theme of a positive double, which author Frederick van Rensselaer Dey (1861–1922) called your "plus-entity." In Dey's brief and oddly compelling instructional tale from 1900, he depicts the life of a down-and-out 17th-century craftsman who discovers that a haunting Presence, or other self, is hovering around his periphery. Dey's hero finds that his counter-self is a real part of him, one that is "calm, steadfast, and self-reliant." As soon as he comes to identify, literally, with his plus-entity, his life is happily transformed. "Make a daily and nightly companion of your plus-entity," the hero counsels.

Introduction

As it happens, the author Dey's life was less than happy: After a middling and prolific career writing pulp crime fiction, including the popular Nick Carter detective tales, the wearied writer shot himself to death in 1922. He left behind a stoic suicide note, asking only that his older brother be taken care of. Dey's widow, Haryot Holt Dey, was herself a notable writer and suffragist who lived until 1950. To use the terms of Dey's own allegory, the author succumbed to his "minus-entity."

How can you get in touch with your stronger plus-entity?

Dress the Part

Never neglect the power of simple things. The manner in which you dress and comport yourself has tremendous impact on your psyche. Most people instinctively sense this without fully acting on it. (This is one reason why the process of transitioning can feel enormously liberating to a transgender person.) Become a thespian, trying out, perhaps subtly at first, different styles of dress, makeup, accessories, and body art. In one of my favorite episodes of *The Simpsons*, a teacher tells young Lisa, "Being tough comes from the inside. First step—change your outside." It's a joke, of course, but like most jokes, it conceals a core truth.

Feed Your Other Self

Allow yourself to become immersed in music, movies, and media that feed your sense of power and self-agency. As an example, consider the elegant but deadly robot named David in the 2012 science fiction movie *Prometheus*; take note of how David studiously models his persona after the cinematic *Lawrence of Arabia*.

Introduction

Although brief, these scenes are no passing trifle; they are mini-models of the kinds of self-making that we all engage in, sometimes without awareness.

Talk Like It

Consider the manner in which you speak. I once knew a crime reporter at a newspaper in upstate New York who had a slight build and appearance—but he spoke in a commanding, self-confident bass voice. It earned him the respect of the police and his newsroom colleagues. Whether natural or affected (I could never tell), his voice altered his entire persona.

Find a Manifesto

You may question the value of reading *The Magic Story* given its author's tragic end. Do not be deterred. Read it tonight. Make its lessons your own. Dey possessed a keen instinct for human nature, including its shadowy and occultic paths to power. If this book doesn't speak to you (although I suspect it will), select another from the works I've mentioned, or find ones of your own.

Stand for Something

The chief cause of mediocrity is purposelessness. We are never more aroused, sensitive, and capable than when we are striving for something. What are you striving for? A watch-the-clock job and entertainment won't bring out more than your most average traits. Above all, you must find a chief aim in life. You should never be embarrassed by your aim. Your aim can be public or intimate. It requires no one's approval—it must be uniquely your own. The only tragedy is not having one.

Introduction

———— ⚭ ————

*   *   *

Since earliest childhood, you have probably felt, as I have, that you are two selves. Be guided by the principle of *The Magic Story*: select the self that builds you. It represents a more powerful choice than may at first appear.

Mitch Horowitz is a PEN Award-winning historian whose books include *Occult America*; *The Miracle Club*; and the G&D titles *The Miracle Habits* and *The Miracle Month*.
Twitter: @MitchHorowitz
Instagram: @MitchHorowitz23

❧ Preface

This wonderful little story, written by Frederick van Rensselaer Dey, first appeared in the December, 1900, and January, 1901, issues of *Success Magazine*. It created an immediate sensation, and urgent requests were made for its reprint in book form. A small edition of a little silver-gray book was published to meet these requests, and this, the First Edition, has virtually disappeared from sight. The fact that the publishers of *Success Magazine* are in almost daily receipt of requests for additional copies is sufficient evidence of the value placed by the holders of the original edition upon the copies in their possession, and of their desire to bring it to the attention of their friends; and the demand has now become so insistent as to lead to the production of this, the Second Edition.

Mr. Dey has woven into this story, in a remarkably effective way, some of the fundamental principles of the "New Thought Movement" which is sweeping over this country, and it is safe to say that the application of these principles, as outlined in the "Magic Story," will accomplish almost, if not quite, all that is herein claimed for them towards the upbuilding and development of a manly, self-reliant, *success-compelling* spirit.

—THE PUBLISHERS

PART
ONE

I WAS sitting alone in the *café*, and had just reached for the sugar preparatory to putting it into my coffee. Outside, the weather was hideous. Snow and sleet came swirling down, and the wind howled frightfully. Every time the outer door opened, a draft of unwelcome air penetrated the uttermost corners of the room. Still, I was comfortable. The snow and sleet and wind conveyed nothing to me except an abstract thanksgiving that I was where it could not affect me. While I dreamed and sipped my coffee, the door opened and closed, and admitted— Sturtevant.

Sturtevant was an undeniable failure, but, withal, an artist of more than ordinary talent. He had, however, fallen into the rut traveled by ne'er-do-wells, and was out at the elbows as well as insolvent.

As I raised my eyes to Sturtevant's, I was conscious of mild surprise at the change in his appearance. Yet he was not dressed differently. He wore the same threadbare coat in which he always appeared, and the old brown hat was the same. And yet there was something new and strange in his appearance. As he swished his hat around to relieve it of the burden of snow deposited by the howling nor'wester, there was something new in the gesticulation. I could not remember when I had invited Sturtevant to dine with me, but involuntarily I beckoned to him. He nodded, and presently seated himself opposite to me. I asked him what he would have, and he, after scanning the bill of fare carelessly, ordered from it leisurely, and invited me to join him in coffee for two. I watched him in stupid wonder, but, as I had invited the obligation, I was prepared to pay for it, although I knew I hadn't sufficient cash to settle the bill. Meanwhile, I noted the brightness of his usual lackluster eyes, and the healthful, hopeful glow upon his cheek, with increasing amazement.

"Have you lost a rich uncle?" I asked.

"No," he replied, calmly, "but I have found my mascot."

"Brindle bull, or terrier?" I inquired.

"Currier," said Sturtevant, at length, pausing with his coffee cup half way to his lips, "I see that I have surprised you. It is not strange, for I am a surprise to myself. I am a new man, a different man,—and the alteration has taken place in the last few hours. You have seen me come into this place broke' many a time, when you have turned away, so that I would think you did not see me. I knew why you did that. It was not because you did not want to pay for a dinner, but because you did not have the money to do it. Is that your check? Let me have it. Thank you. I haven't any money with me to-night, but I,—well, this is my treat."

He called the waiter to him, and, with an inimitable flourish, signed his name on the backs of the two checks, and waved him away. After that he was silent a moment while he looked into my eyes, smiling at the astonishment which I in vain strove to conceal.

Part One

※

"Do you know an artist who possesses more talent than I?" he asked, presently. "No. Do you happen to know anything in the line of my profession that I could not accomplish, if I applied myself to it? No. You have been a reporter on the dailies for—how many?—seven or eight years. Do you remember when I ever had any credit until to-night? No. Was I refused just now? You have seen for yourself. To-morrow my new career begins. Within a month I shall have a bank account. Why? Because I have discovered the secret of success."

"Yes," he continued, when I did not reply, "my fortune is made. I have been reading a strange story, and, since reading it, I feel that my fortune is assured. It will make your fortune, too. All you have to do is to read it. You have no idea what it will do for you. Nothing is impossible after you know that story. It makes everything as plain as A, B, C. The very instant you grasp its true meaning, success is certain. This morning I was a hopeless, aimless bit of garbage in the metropolitan ash can; to-night I wouldn't change places with a millionaire. That sounds foolish, but it is true. The millionaire has spent his enthusiasm; mine is all at hand."

"You amaze me," I said, wondering if he had been drinking absinthe. "Won't you tell me the story? I should like to hear it."

"Certainly. I mean to tell it to the whole world. It is really remarkable that it should have been written and should remain in print so long, with never a soul to appreciate it until now. This morning I was starving. I hadn't any credit, nor a place to get a meal. I was seriously meditating suicide. I had gone to three of the papers for which I had done work, and had been handed back all that I had submitted. I had to choose quickly between death by suicide and death slowly by starvation. Then I found the story and read it. You can hardly imagine the transformation. Why, my dear boy, everything changed at once—and there you are."

"But what is the story, Sturtevant?"

"Wait; let me finish. I took those same old drawings to other editors, and every one of them was accepted at once."

"Can the story do for others what it has done for you ? For example, would it be of assistance to me?" I asked.

"Help you? why not? Listen and I will tell it to you, although, really, you should read it. Still, I will tell it as best I can. It is like this: you see—," The waiter interrupted us at that moment. He informed Sturtevant that he was wanted at the telephone, and, with a word of apology, the artist left the table. Five minutes later I saw him rush out into the sleet and wind and disappear. Within the recollection of the frequenters of that *café*, Sturtevant had never before been called out by telephone. That, of itself, was substantial proof of a change in his circumstances.

One night, on the street, I encountered Avery, a former college chum, then a reporter on one of the evening papers. It was about a month after my memorable interview with Sturtevant, which, by that time, was almost forgotten.

"Hello, old chap," he said; "how's the world using you? Still on space?"

"Yes," I replied, bitterly, "with prospects of being on the town, shortly. But you look as if things were coming your way. Tell me all about it."

"Things have been coming my way, for a fact, and it is all remarkable, when all is said. You know Sturtevant, don't you? It's all due to him. I was plumb down on my luck—thinking of the morgue and all that—looking for you, in fact, with the idea that you would lend me enough to pay my room rent, when I met Sturtevant. He told me a story, and, really, old man, it is the most remarkable story you ever heard; it made a new man of me. Within twenty-four hours I was on my feet, and I've hardly known a care or a trouble since."

Avery's statement, uttered calmly, and with the air of one who had merely pronounced an axiom, recalled to my mind the conversation with Sturtevant in the *café* that stormy night, nearly a month before.

"It must be a remarkable story," I said, incredulously. "Sturtevant mentioned it to me once. I have not seen him since. Where is he now?"

"He has been making war sketches in Cuba, at two hundred a week; he's just returned. It is a fact that everybody that has heard that story has done well since. There are Cosgrove and Phillips—friends of mine—you don't know them. One's a real estate agent; the other a broker's clerk. Sturtevant told them the story, and they have experienced the same result that I have; and they are not the only ones, either."

"Do you know the story?" I asked. "Will you try its effect on me?"

"Certainly; with the greatest pleasure in the world. I would like to have it printed in big black type, and posted on the elevated stations throughout New York. It certainly would do a lot of good, and it's as simple as A, B, C; like living on a farm. Excuse me a minute, will you ? I see Danforth over there. Back in a minute, old chap."

He nodded and smiled,—and was gone. I saw him join the man whom he had designated as Danforth. My attention was distracted for a moment, and, when I looked again, both had disappeared.

If the truth be told, I was hungry. My pocket at that moment contained exactly five cents; just enough to pay my fare uptown, but insufficient also to stand the expense of filling my stomach. There was a "night owl" wagon in the neighborhood, where I had frequently "stood up" the purveyor of midnight dainties, and to him I applied. He was leaving the wagon as I was on the point of entering it, and I accosted him.

"I'm broke again," I said, with extreme cordiality. "You'll have to trust me once more. Some ham and eggs, I think, will do for the present."

He coughed, hesitated a moment, and then re-entered the wagon with me.

"Mr. Currier is good for anything he orders," he said to the man in charge; "one of my old customers. This is Mr. Bryan, Mr. Currier. He will take good care of you, and 'stand for' you, just the same as I would. The fact is, I have sold out. I've just turned over the outfit to Bryan. By the way, isn't Mr. Sturtevant a friend of yours?"

I nodded. I couldn't have spoken if I had tried.

"Well," continued the ex-night-owl man, "he came here one night, about a month ago, and told me the most wonderful story I ever heard. I've just bought a place in Eighth Avenue, where I am going to run a regular restaurant—near Twenty-third Street. Come and see me." He was out of the wagon, and the sliding door had been banged shut before I could stop him; so I ate my ham and eggs in silence, and resolved that I would hear that story before I slept. In fact, I began to regard it with superstition. If it had made so many fortunes, surely it should be capable of making mine.

The certainty that the wonderful story—I began to regard it as magic—was in the air, possessed me. As I started to walk homeward, fingering the solitary nickel in my pocket and contemplating the certainty of riding down town in the morning, I experienced the sensation of something stealthily pursuing me, as if Fate were treading along behind me, yet never overtaking, and I was conscious that I was possessed with or by the story. When I reached Union Square, I examined my address book for the home of Sturtevant. It was not recorded there. Then I remembered the *café* in University Place, and, although the hour was late, it occurred to me that he might be there.

He was! In a far corner of the room, surrounded by a group of acquaintances, I saw him. He discovered me at the same instant, and motioned to me to join them at the table. There was no chance for the story, however. There were half a dozen around the table, and I was the farthest removed from Sturtevant. But I kept my eyes upon him, and bided my time, determined that, when he rose to depart, I would go with him. A silence, suggestive of respectful awe, had fallen upon the party when I took my seat. Every one seemed to be thinking, and the attention of all was fixed upon Sturtevant. The cause was apparent. He had been telling the story. I had entered the *café* just too late to hear it. On my right, when I took my seat, was a doctor; on my left a law-

lows, and it 'braced them up,' as it had me. It seems incredible that a mere story can have such a tonic effect upon the success of so many persons who are engaged in such widely different occupations, but that is what it has done. It is a kind of never failing remedy, like a cough mixture that is warranted to cure everything, from a cold in the head to galloping consumption. There was Parsons, for example. He is a broker, you know, and had been on the wrong side of the market for a month. He had utterly lost his grip, and was on the verge of failure. I happened to meet him at the time he was feeling the bluest, and, before we parted, something brought me around to the subject of the story, and I related it to him. It had the same effect upon him that it had on me, and has had upon everybody who has heard it, as far as I know. I think you will all agree with me, that it is not the story itself that performs the surgical operation on the minds of those who are familiar with it; it is the way it is told—in print, I mean. The author has, somehow, produced a psychological effect which is indescribable. The reader is hypnotized. He receives a mental and moral tonic. Perhaps, doctor, you can give some scientific explanation of the influence exerted by the story. It is a sort of elixir manufactured out of words, eh?"

From that the company entered upon a general discussion of theories. Now and then slight references were made to the story itself, and they were just sufficient to tantalize me—the only one present who had not heard it.

At length, I left my chair, and, passing around the table, seized Sturtevant by one arm, and succeeded in drawing him away from the party.

The Magic Story

"If you have any consideration for an old friend who is rapidly being driven mad by the existence of that confounded story, which Fate seems determined that I shall never hear, you will relate it to me now," I said, savagely.

Sturtevant stared at me in mild surprise.

"All right," he said. "The others will excuse me for a few moments, I think. Sit down here, and you shall have it. I found it pasted in an old scrapbook I purchased in Ann Street, for three cents; and there isn't a thing about it by which one can get any idea in what publication it originally appeared, or who wrote it. When I discovered it, I began casually to read it, and in a moment I was interested. Before I left it, I had read it through many times, so that I could repeat it almost word for word. It affected me strangely—as if I had come in contact with some strong personality. There seems to be in the story a personal element that applies to every one who reads it. Well, after I had read it several times, I began to think it over. I couldn't stay in the house, so I seized my coat and hat and went out. I must have walked several miles, buoyantly, without realizing that I was the same man who, only a short time before, had been in the depths of despondency. That was the day I met you here—you remember."

We were interrupted at that instant by a uniformed messenger, who handed Sturtevant a telegram. It was from his chief, and demanded his instant attendance at the office. The messenger had already been delayed an hour, and there was no help for it; he must go at once.

"Too bad!" said Sturtevant, rising and extending his hand. "Tell you what I'll do, old chap. I'm not likely to be gone any more than an hour or two. You take my key and wait for me in my room. In the *escritoire* near the window you will find an old scrap-book, bound in rawhide. It was manufactured, I have no doubt, by the author of the magic story. Wait for me in my room until I return."

With that he went out, and I lost no time in taking advantage of the permission he had given me.

I found the book without difficulty. It was a quaint, home-made affair, covered, as Sturtevant had said, with rawhide, and bound with leather thongs. The pages formed an odd combination of yellow paper, vellum and home-made parchment. I found the story, curiously printed on the last-named material. It was quaint and strange. Evidently, the printer had "set" it under the supervision of the writer. The phraseology was an unusual combination of seventeenth and eighteenth century mannerisms, and the interpolation of italics and capitals could have originated in no other brain than that of its author.

In reproducing the following story, the peculiarities of type, spelling, etc., are eliminated, but in other respects it remains unchanged.

Nothing worth while is attainable without effort. By the same token, a thoughtful reading of "The Magic Story" and a correct interpretation of its "lessons" are essential to a full appreciation of its inspirational value.

The author has woven into this story in a remarkably effective way the basic principles of a successful life, and it is safe to say that per-

*sistent application of these princi-
ples will accomplish almost, if not
quite, all that is claimed for them
in the development of a self-reliant,
success-compelling spirit.*

*Enthusiastic readers of this
unusual book, appreciating its inspir-
iting force, give it generous publicity,
and as a result its sphere of influence
is being constantly enlarged.*

PART
TWO

In the Old Scrap Book

INASMUCH as I have evolved from my experience the one great secret of success for all worldly undertakings, I deem it wise, now that the number of my days is nearly counted, to give to the generations that are to follow me the benefit of whatsoever knowledge I possess. I do not apologize for the manner of my expression, nor for lack of literary merit, the latter being, I wot, its own apology. Tools much heavier than the pen have been my portion, and, moreover, the weight of years has somewhat palsied hand and brain; nevertheless, the fact I can tell, and that I deem the meat within the nut. What mattereth it, in what manner the shell be broken, so that the meat be obtained and rendered useful? I doubt not that I shall use, in the telling, expressions that have clung to my memory since childhood; for, when men attain the number of my years, happenings of youth are like to be clearer to their perceptions than are events of recent date; nor doth it matter much how a thought is expressed, if it be wholesome and helpful, and findeth the understanding.

Much have I wearied my brain anent the question, how best to describe this recipe for success that I have discovered, and it seemeth advisable to give it as it came to me; that is, if I relate somewhat of the story of my life, the directions for agglomerating the substances, and supplying the seasoning for the accomplishment of the dish, will plainly be perceived. Happen they may; and that men may be born generations after I am dust, who will live to bless me for the words I write.

My father, then, was a seafaring man who, early in life, forsook his vocation, and settled on a plantation in the colony of Virginia, where, some years thereafter, I was born, which event took place in the year 1642; and that was over a hundred years ago. Better for my father had it been had he hearkened to the wise advice of my mother, that he remain in the calling of his education; but he would not have it so, and the good vessel he captained was bartered for the land I spoke of. Here beginneth the first lesson to be acquired:

Man should not be blinded to whatso-ever merit exists in the opportunity which he hath in hand, remember-ing that a thousand promises for the future should weigh as naught against the possession of a single piece of silver.

When I had achieved ten years, my mother's soul took flight, and two years thereafter my worthy father followed her. I, being their only begotten, was left alone; howbeit, there were friends who, for a time, cared for me; that is to say, they offered me a home beneath their roof,—a thing which I took advantage of for the space of five months. From my father's estate there came to me naught; but, in the wisdom that came with increasing years, I convinced myself that his friend, under whose roof I lingered for some time, had defrauded him, and therefore me.

Of the time from the age of twelve and a half until I was three and twenty, I will make no recital here, since that time hath naught to do with this tale; but some time after, having in my possession the sum of sixteen guineas, ten, which I had saved from the fruits of my labor, I took ship to Boston town, where I began work first as a cooper, and thereafter as a ship's carpenter, although always after the craft was docked; for the sea was not amongst my desires.

Fortune will sometimes smile upon an intended victim because of pure perversity of temper. Such was one of my experiences. I prospered, and, at seven and twenty, owned the yard wherein, less than four years earlier, I had worked for hire. Fortune, howbeit, is a jade who must be coerced; she will not be coddled. Here beginneth the second lesson to be acquired:

Fortune is ever elusive, and can only be retained by force. Deal with her tenderly and she will forsake you for a stronger man. [In that, methinks, she is not unlike other women of my knowledge.]

About this time, Disaster (which is one of the heralds of broken spirits and lost resolve), paid me a visit. Fire ravaged my yards, leaving nothing in its blackened paths but debts, which I had not the coin wherewith to defray. I labored with my acquaintances, seeking assistance for a new start, but the fire that had burned my competence seemed also to have consumed their sympathies. So it happened, within a short time, that not only had I lost all, but I was hopelessly indebted to others; and for that they cast me into prison. It is possible that I might have rallied from my losses but for this last indignity, which broke down my spirits so that I became utterly despondent. Upward of a year was I detained within the gaol; and, when I did come forth, it was not the same hopeful, happy man, content with his lot, and with confidence in the world and its people, who had entered there.

Life has many pathways, and of them by far the greater number lead downward. Some are precipitous, others are less abrupt; but ultimately, no matter at what inclination the angle may be fixed, they arrive at the same destination—failure. And here beginneth the third lesson:

The Magic Story

Failure exists only in the grave. Man, being alive, hath not yet failed; always he may turn about and ascend by the same path he descended by; and there may be one that is less abrupt (albeit longer of achievement), and more adaptable to his condition.

When I came forth from prison, I was penniless. In all the world I possessed naught beyond the poor garments which covered me, and a walking stick which the turnkey had permitted me to retain, since it was worthless. Being a skilled workman, howbeit, I speedily found employment at good wages; but, having eaten of the fruit of worldly advantage, dissatisfaction possessed me. I became morose and sullen; whereat, to cheer my spirits, and for the sake of forgetting the

losses I had sustained, I passed my eve-
nings at the tavern. Not that I drank over-
much of liquor, except on occasion (for I
have ever been somewhat abstemious),
but that I could laugh, and sing, and parry
wit and badinage with my ne'er-do-well
companions; and here might be included
the fourth lesson:

*Seek comrades among the industri-
ous, for those who are idle will sap
your energies from you.*

It was my pleasure at that time to
relate, upon slight provocation, the tale of
my disasters, and to rail against the men
whom I deemed to have wronged me,
because they had seen fit not to come to
my aid. Moreover, I found childish delight
in filching from my employer, each day,
a few moments of the time for which he

paid me. Such a thing is less honest than downright theft.

This habit continued and grew upon me until the day dawned which found me not only without employment, but also without character, which meant that I could not hope to find work with any other employer in Boston town.

It was then that I regarded myself a failure. I can liken my condition at that time for naught more similar than that of a man who, descending the steep side of a mountain, loses his foothold. The farther he slides, the faster he goes. I have also heard this condition described by the word Ishmaelite, which I understand to be a man whose hand is against everybody, and who thinks that the hands of every other man are against him; and here beginneth the fifth lesson:

Part Two

The Ishmaelite and the leper are the same, since both are abominations in the sight of man—albeit they differ much, in that the former may be restored to perfect health. The former is entirely the result of imagination; the latter has poison in his blood.

I will not discourse at length upon the gradual degeneration of my energies. It is not meet ever to dwell much upon misfortunes (which saying is also worthy of remembrance). It is enough if I add that the day came when I possessed naught wherewith to purchase food and raiment, and I found myself like unto a pauper, save at infrequent times when I could earn a few pence, or, mayhap, a shilling. Steady employment I could not secure, so I became emaciated in body, and naught but a skeleton in spirit.

The Magic Story

My condition, then, was deplorable; not so much for the body, be it said, as for the mental part of me, which was sick unto death. In my imagination I deemed myself ostracised by the whole world, for I had sunk very low indeed; and here beginneth the sixth and final lesson to be acquired (which cannot be told in one sentence, nor in one paragraph, but must needs be adapted from the remainder of this tale).

Well do I remember my awakening, for it came in the night, when, in truth, I did awake from sleep. My bed was a pile of shavings in the rear of the cooper shop where once I had worked for hire; my roof was the pyramid of casks, underneath which I had established myself. The night was cold, and I was chilled, albeit, paradoxically, I had been dreaming of light and warmth and of the repletion of

Moreover, it was not the dream itself which affected me; it was the impression made by it, and the influence that it exerted over me, which accomplished my enfranchisement. In a word, then, I encouraged my other identity. After toiling through a tempest of snow and wind, I peered into a window and saw that other being. He was rosy with health; before him, on the hearth, blazed a fire of logs; there was conscious power and force in his demeanor; he was physically and mentally muscular. I rapped timidly upon the door, and he bade me enter. There was a not unkindly smile of derision in his eyes as he motioned me to a chair by the fire; but he uttered no word of welcome; and, when I had warmed myself, I went forth again into the tempest, burdened with the shame which the contrast between us had forced upon me. It was then that I awoke; and here cometh the strange part of my tale, for, when I did awake, I was not alone. There was a Presence with me; intangible to others, I discovered later, but real to me.

The Presence was in my likeness, yet was it strikingly unlike. The brow, not more lofty than my own, yet seemed more round and full; the eyes, clear, direct, and filled with purpose, glowed with enthusiasm and resolution; the lips, chin—ay, the whole contour of face and figure was dominant and determined.

He was calm, steadfast, and self-reliant; I was cowering, filled with nervous trembling, and fearsome of intangible shadows. When the Presence turned away, I followed, and throughout the day I never lost sight of it, save when it disappeared for a time beyond some doorway where I dared not enter; at such places, I awaited its return with trepidation and awe, for I could not help wondering at the temerity of the Presence (so like myself, and yet so unlike), in daring to enter where my own feet feared to tread.

It seemed also, as if purposely I was led to the place and to the men where and before whom I most dreaded to appear; to offices where once I had transacted business; to men with whom I had financial dealings. Throughout the day I pursued the Presence, and at evening saw it disappear beyond the portals of a hostelry famous for its cheer and good living. I sought the pyramid of casks and shavings.

Not again in my dreams that night did I encounter the Better Self (for that is what I have named it), albeit, when, perchance, I awakened from slumber, it was near to me, ever wearing that calm smile of kindly derision which could not be mistaken for pity, nor for condolence in any form. The contempt of it stung me sorely.

The second day was not unlike the first, being a repetition of its forerunner, and I was again doomed to wait outside during the visits which the Presence paid to places where I fain would have gone had I possessed the requisite courage. It is fear which deporteth a man's soul from his body and rendereth it a thing to be despised. Many a time I essayed to address it, but enunciation rattled in my throat, unintelligible; and the day closed like its predecessor.

This happened many days, one following another, until I ceased to count them; albeit, I discovered that constant association with the Presence was producing an effect upon me; and one night, when I awoke among the casks and discerned that he was present, I made bold to speak, albeit with marked timidity.

"Who are you?" I ventured to ask; and I was startled into an upright posture by the sound of my own voice; and the question seemed to give pleasure to my companion, so that I fancied there was less of derision in his smile when he responded.

"I am that I am," was the reply. "I am he who you have been; I am he who you may be again; wherefore do you hesitate? I am he who you were, and whom you have cast out for other company. I am the man made in the image of God, who once possessed your body. Once we dwelt within it together, not in harmony, for that can never be, nor yet in unity, for that is impossible, but as tenants in common who rarely fought for full possession. Then you were a puny thing, but you became selfish and exacting until I could no longer abide with you, wherefore I stepped out. There is a plus-entity and a minus-entity in every human body that is born into the world. Whichever one of these is favored by the flesh becomes dominant; then is the other inclined to abandon its habitation, temporarily or for all time. I am the plus-entity of yourself; you are the minus-entity. I own all things; you possess naught. That body which we both inhabited is mine, but it is unclean, and I will not dwell within it. Cleanse it, and I will take possession.

"Why do you pursue me?" I next asked the Presence.

"You have pursued me, not I you. You can exist without me for a time, but your path leads downward, and the end is death. Now that you approach the end, you debate if it be not politic that you should cleanse your house and invite me to enter. Step aside, then, from the brain and the will; cleanse them of your presence; only on that condition will I ever occupy them again."

"The brain hath lost its power," I faltered. "The will is a weak thing, now; can you repair them?"

"Listen!" said the Presence, and he towered over me while I cowered abjectly at his feet. "To the plus-entity of a man, all things are possible. The world belongs to him—is his estate. He fears naught, dreads naught, stops at naught; he asks no privileges, but demands them; he *dominates*, and cannot cringe; his requests are orders; opposition flees at his approach; he levels mountains, fills in vales, and travels on an even plane where stumbling is unknown."

Thereafter, I slept again, and, when I awoke, I seemed to be in a different world. The sun was shining and I was conscious that birds twittered above my head. My body, yesterday trembling and uncertain, had become vigorous and filled with energy. I gazed upon the pyramid of casks in amazement that I had so long made use of it for an abiding place, and I was wonderingly conscious that I had passed my last night beneath its shelter.

The events of the night recurred to me, and I looked about me for the Presence. It was not visible. But anon I discovered, cowering in a far corner of my resting place, a puny, abject, shuddering figure, distorted of visage, deformed of shape, disheveled and unkempt of appearance. It tottered as it walked, for it approached me piteously; but I laughed aloud, mercilessly. Perchance I knew then that it was the minus-entity, and that the plus-entity was within me; albeit I did not then realize it. Moreover,

I was in haste to get away; I had no time for philosophy. There was much for me to do—much; strange it was that I had not thought of that yesterday. But yesterday was gone—to-day was with me—it had just begun.

As had once been my daily habit, I turned my steps in the direction of the tavern where formerly I had partaken of my meals. I nodded cheerily as I entered, and smiled in recognition of returned salutations. Men who had ignored me for months bowed graciously when I passed them on the thoroughfare. I went to the washroom, and from there to the breakfast table; afterwards, when I passed the taproom, I paused a moment and said to the landlord:

"I will occupy the same room that I formerly used, if, perchance, you

have it at disposal. If not, another will do as well, until I can obtain it."

Then I went out and hurried with all haste to the cooperage. There was a huge wain in the yard, and men were loading it with casks for shipment. I asked no questions, but, seizing barrels, began hurling them to the men who worked atop of the load. When this was finished, I entered the shop. There was a vacant bench; I recognized its disuse by the litter on its top. It was the same at which I had once worked. Stripping off my coat, I soon cleared it of *impedimenta*. In a moment more I was seated, with my foot on the vice-lever, shaving staves.

It was an hour later when the master workman entered the room, and he paused in surprise at sight of me; already there was a goodly pile of neatly shaven staves beside me, for in those days I was an excellent workman; there was none better, but, alas! now, age hath deprived me of my skill. I replied to his unasked question with the brief but comprehensive sentence: "I have returned to work, sir." He nodded his head and passed on, viewing the work of other men, albeit anon he glanced askance in my direction.

Here endeth the sixth and last lesson to be acquired, although there is more to be said, since from that moment I was a successful man, and ere long possessed another shipyard, and had acquired a full competence of worldly goods.

I pray you who read, heed well the following admonitions, since upon them depend the word "success" and all that it implies:

Part Two

——— ❧ ———

Whatsoever you desire of good is yours. You have but to stretch forth your hand and take it.

Learn that the consciousness of dominant power within you is the possession of all things attainable.

Have no fear of any sort or shape, for fear is an adjunct of the minus-entity.

If you have skill, apply it; the world must profit by it, and, therefore, you.

Make a daily and nightly companion of your plus-entity; if you heed its advice, you cannot go wrong.

Remember, philosophy is an argument; the world, which is your property, is an accumulation of facts.

Go, therefore, and do that which is within you to do; take no heed of gestures which would beckon you aside; *ask of no man permission to perform.*

The minus-entity requests favors; the plus-entity grants them. Fortune waits upon every footstep you take; seize her, bind her, hold her, for she is yours; she belongs to you.

Start out now, with these admonitions in your mind. Stretch out your hand, and grasp the plus, which, maybe, you have never made use of, save in grave emergencies. Life is an emergency most grave.

Your plus-entity is beside you now; cleanse your brain, and strengthen your will. It will take possession. It waits upon you.

Start to-night; start now upon this new journey.

Be always on your guard. Whichever entity controls you, the other hovers at your side; beware lest the evil enter, even for a moment.

Part Two

My task is done. I have written the recipe for "success." If followed, it cannot fail. Wherein I may not be entirely comprehended, the plus-entity of whosoever reads will supply the deficiency; and upon that Better Self of mine, I place the burden of imparting to generations that are to come, the secret of this all-pervading good—*the secret of being what you have it within you to be.*

[THE END]

Dey took up story writing for amusement while convalescing from a serious illness, and later made it his life work. His first full-length story was written for Beadle and Adams in 1881.

In 1891, Street & Smith hired him to continue a series of novelettes, begun by John R. Coryell, relating the adventures of a detective named Nick Carter. Most of his Nick Carter stories appeared under the pseudonyms "A Celebrated Author" and "The Author of 'Nick Carter.'" It is said that Dey wrote between one thousand and eleven hundred Nick Carter stories, comprising over forty million words, all written longhand. Besides these he wrote more serious books and serials. Two of his earlier books, before his dime-novel days, "The Magic Word" and "The Magic Story," written in 1899, were extremely popular and passed through some twenty editions.

About the Author

He also wrote stories, of various kinds, as by Rose Beckman, Marmaduke Dey, Frederick Ormund, Dirck Van Doren, Varick Venardy, and under many other names, including the House Name Bertha M. Clay. It is highly unlikely that his bibliography will ever be fully established, so that his importance for the nineteenth-century American literature of the fantastic is more a matter of assertion than sure knowledge. Writing as "Varick Vanardy," he created "The Night Wind," who appeared in stories from 1913 to the early 1920s.

Dey also worked in the newspaper industry as a police reporter, general reporter, special correspondent, and at various editorial desks.

He was twice married; first to Annie Shepard, of Providence, R. I., June 4, 1885, by whom he had two children and which ended in divorce, and second to Mrs. Hattie (Hamblin) Cahoon, April 1, 1898. The second Mrs. Dey was herself an author, writing under the name "Haryot Holt Dey."

Dey had a very vivid imagination. A writer in the St. Louis Post-Dispatch said:

Dey, like Harbaugh, had an incorrigible imagination. It made him famous as a writer, but it also had its penalties. . . . He had always indulged a penchant for playing that he was a millionaire and spent his money accordingly. He would pose as a wealthy sportsman, a rich California fruit-grower, a millionaire railroad official any fiction that seemed to lend glamour to his momentary position was not beyond the reach of his voracious imagination. As for the expense of his posing, that didn't matter. It was worth any price to him just to be regarded for a few minutes as the romantic figure he sought to impersonate.

Dey was always purchasing estates and never completing the transactions. Once he had $200 in his pocket and it was all he had in the world. But he went over to the Erie Basin posing as a millionaire and after looking over several yachts, picked out a craft worth somewhere in the neighborhood of $100,000, and gave the $200 as evidence of good faith to clinch the option until he could arrange the terms of the contract. The dreamer had just those few minutes of being looked upon and pointed out as the purchaser of a yacht. . . .

* * *

Two decades later Dey was broke. With no market for his stories after the era of the dime-novel had ended, Dey could see no way of making a living and he committed suicide. Dey shot himself in his room in the Hotel Broztell in New York City, during the night of April 25, 1922 or the morning of April 26, 1922.

Before he killed himself he wrote to a friend telling him of what he intended to do. The friend got the letter and hastened to the little hotel where the "Colonel" was staying. As he had not registered under his own name, the visitor could not locate him and described him to the clerk.

"That description fits a gentleman on the seventh floor," said the clerk, "but surely he had no thought of suicide. The man is a wealthy fruit grower in California. Why, last night before he went up to his room, he offered me a position in the fruit business in California."

"That's the man I am looking for," said his friend.

And it was. The hotel clerk was likely the last human being Dey spoke to on earth. Dey had just posted a letter telling his friend that "everything had gone to smash and he belonged with it" and that he "couldn't stand the gaff," and then on his way up to his room, which as likely as not he couldn't pay for, he stopped to offer the clerk a job on his fruit ranch in California.

Sad though the end of Dey's life turned out to be he did, at least, have a profound understanding of the power of the human imagination—as is evidenced by *The Magic Story*. Such a tremendous imagination as this it was that lay at the root of his success as a story teller. In the end, however, it failed him. He couldn't dream up an answer to his predicament. Maybe he'd just had enough . . . But that doesn't stop all of us taking inspiration from his work, which was truly great.